P9-DDW-367

PLAYS FOR PERFORMANCE

A series designed for
contemporary production and study
Edited by
Nicholas Rudall and Bernard Sahlins

SOPHOCLES

Antigone

*In a New Translation by
Nicholas Rudall*

Ivan R. Dee
CHICAGO

Library of Congress Cataloging-in-Publication Data:
Sophocles.
    [Antigone. English]
    Antigone / Sophocles ; in a new translation by Nicholas Rudall.
      p. cm.
    ISBN 1–56663–210–2 (alk. paper). —
    ISBN 1–56663–211–0 (pbk. : alk. paper)
    1. Antigone (Greek mythology)—Drama. I. Rudall, Nicholas. II. Title.
PA4414.A7R84   1998
882'.01—dc21   98–29136

INTRODUCTION

by Nicholas Rudall

The *Antigone* was written in 441 B.C. when Sophocles was in his mid-fifties. Although it is clearly the work of an artist at the height of his powers, it is nonetheless the earliest of the so-called Theban plays. *Oedipus the King* was written some fifteen years later, and *Oedipus at Colonus* perhaps in 406 B.C. The fact that all three plays focus on Thebes is simply an accident of the geography of the compelling story of the house of Oedipus. But it is an accident that Sophocles exploits for its contemporary historical reverberations. Thebes was the only Greek city to side with the Persians in the then-recent Persian Wars. Its politics were therefore suspect to the Greeks and easily associated with the excesses of Eastern despotism. And one of the major themes of the *Antigone* is the excessive use of his power by the new tyrant, Creon.

But this play was performed at Athens, and its arguments were directed at Athenians. Much of the force of Creon's downfall would not have been lost upon the more self-reflective of the Athenian audience. Athens, though an often self-congratulatory democracy, was, when the play was written, exercising a virtually despotic rule over its so-called allies, its friends, its political *family*. Sophocles' warning had currency then and has retained its power since.

The Plot

The play is meticulously structured. It begins with a succinct and powerful prologue between Antigone and her sister Ismene. We learn of the death of their two brothers. We learn that Creon will bury Eteocles and deny burial to Polyneices. But most important we are thrust into the essence of the play: loyalty to one's family versus loyalty to the state. The loyalty to one's family is underlined by the raising of the important issue of divine law versus human law. For a modern audience it is important that the burial of Polyneices be seen as part of a set of human rules sanctioned by the gods. One has only to recall the importance of the recovery of the dead in the *Iliad* to enter into the appropriate historical consciousness. Burial of the dead was an inescapable duty of the living. To deny burial was to deny eternal rest. To deny burial was to deny an ancient and unwritten law of the gods.

But that is what Creon does in his decree. The Chorus of elders have celebrated the survival of the city but are circumspect about this decree. The Watchman serves two important dramatic functions: he is a commoner in a field of princes, and though he is often quite comical he offers a rare glimpse of sober common sense. The arrest of Antigone begins the escalation of Creon's confrontations with his family and finally with his own institutions. He argues with Antigone and Ismene. He berates his son, Haimon. He is implacable once more toward Antigone. And finally he resists Teiresias, the seer whose gifts have saved the state and helped secure Creon as tyrant. The Chorus travels from indecision and discretion to confrontation and resolution.

4

The central conflict is one of ideas and of character. Antigone believes in the right and duty of her individual conscience. She believes that she has a moral and spiritual obligation to bury her brother. She believes that these necessities outweigh the dictates of mere mortals. She is prepared to die for her beliefs.

Creon believes that the state is the supreme arbiter when it comes to a question of the survival of the body politic. He *is* the state. He believes that he must deny anarchy and support his own rule of law. He is prepared to punish those who defy him with death— even if they are potential members of his family.

Antigone is a richly complex character. She is of course an idealist. Yet she needs the help of others. When she does not get it she is, in her own words, a doer. She will do the deed. She is proud but not perhaps to the point of arrogance. She is certainly tactless in her dealings with the king. Yet she is vulnerable. She does not *seek* death. She loves life and mourns her death because she will die unmarried and childless.

Creon is not to be seen as an implacable tyrant from the start. On the contrary, he has just survived a civil war and its accompanying anarchy. And it must be said that Polyneices, whom he now refuses to bury, was the aggressor in this war. Creon clearly has the good of the state at heart. But he gradually betrays those aspects of a despot that were commonplace on the Greek stage: he begins to suspect everyone of conspiracy. He believes that money is changing hands to ensure his downfall. He becomes quick to anger even with the son he loves. He becomes increasingly stubborn. It must be noted that in the end he sees his error and tries to correct it. But he is too late, and a man who loved his family and his city loses everything.

One of the riches of this play is the counterpoint of male and female. It is beyond the scope of this introduction to dissect its complexity. But it is one of the compelling reasons for mounting a contemporary production. The male sex is the cause of death. Polyneices and Eteocles kill and are killed. Creon effectively is the killer of Haimon, Antigone, and Eurydice. Antigone uses her moral energy to restore a balance. Thereby she is deprived of her natural role of wife and mother. Eurydice, who blames her husband also for the death of a previous son, will be mother no more. The procreative female is stifled by the male. In the end we are left with a city that contains no life and no potential for continuity.

About the Translation

The words of this text are meant to be spoken. Where the Greek is long and sometimes convoluted I have chosen the shorter staccato rhythms of modern English conversation. But apart from the Watchman, who is intentionally colloquial and comic, the overall style is not colloquial. In fact the poetry of the *Antigone* is often dense and peculiarly ornate in its diction. I have tried to make this felt in many ways but most significantly by attempting to individuate the speech patterns of the characters. For example, Creon should sound like an eloquent politician, though beneath the veil of his oratory we should catch glimpses of the ordinary and sometimes bitter human being. Teiresias is a religious devotee whose diction verges on the Gothic. Haimon is eloquent but young, and his language, if not actually naive, is often simpler than his father's. Antigone is the most complicated to render, for she ranges from conversational intimacy with her sister through intellectual vigor in her arguments with Creon to the final lyricism of her departure from the stage and from this earth.

CHARACTERS

ANTIGONE, sister of Eteocles and Polyneices
ISMENE, sister of Antigone
CREON, king of Thebes
HAIMON, son of Creon
TEIRESIAS, a prophet
EURYDICE, wife of Creon
WATCHMAN
MESSENGER
CHORUS of male Theban elders

Antigone

Thebes. Before the palace gate.

ANTIGONE: My sister. My Ismene. We are alive . . . but
the grief, the suffering that Zeus puts on us I
know *must* come from our father's curse.
I have seen it all, the grief, the sense of doom, the
shame, yes, the disgrace, in the eyes of the world.
I have seen it all, your sufferings and mine.
But now the pain gets worse. This edict . . . the
people say that Creon has proclaimed it to the
whole city. What have you heard?
The wickedness of our enemies will soon destroy
our family.
Do you believe me? Do you understand? 10

ISMENE: My sister. My Antigone. I have heard nothing.
Nothing.
Not a word about our friends or family. Not since
that moment when we lost our two brothers—
when our world died as they died, a double
breath, a double death. The Argive army has left.
I have no further news. There is neither good nor
bad in the air.

ANTIGONE: That is why I brought you from the house.
What I have to say is for your ears alone.

ISMENE: Tell me all. I see that you are deeply troubled. 20

ANTIGONE: My trouble is indeed deep. Creon will
honor one of our brothers in death, *dis*honor
the other.

11

Eteocles he has buried, respecting all law, all custom, all sense of justice.

And Eteocles now shares honor with the dead.

But Polyneices is a mere corpse in the sand, a sad dead body that none can bury, none mourn for. Bereft of tears, bereft of soothing earth, his body lies there to fill the hungry eyes and jaws of scavenging birds.

No one shall touch him. Creon has made this a law.

And he, the great Creon, comes here now to proclaim this law to you and me, specifically to *me* . . . and to make its meaning clear to those citizens who know nothing about it. But there is more. . . .

He will condemn to death anyone who attempts to bury Polyneices.

And the death will be by public stoning in the city.

That is the truth. What will you do? Are you as noble as your blood?

Or have you fallen, fallen low?

ISMENE: If this is where matters now lie . . . what can I do?

My poor sister, I can do nothing that will either help or harm.

ANTIGONE: Then will you join with me in what I have to do?

ISMENE: What is it that you have to do, what risk will you take?

ANTIGONE: Will you join with me and bury the body?

ISMENE: Polyneices? . . . but the law forbids . . .

ANTIGONE: He is our brother. Perhaps you wish he was not. *I* will never forsake him.

ISMENE: You are rash, my sister. Creon has passed an edict.

ANTIGONE: Creon cannot keep me from the one I love.

ISMENE: Alas alas. I love you, my sister. But remember how our father died, not only unloved but hated, *hated*. He knew the curse and he put out his own sad eyes.
Remember, my sister, remember his wife, his own mother.
Remember her death, the anguish and the shame. The noose.
Remember the death of brothers.
They murdered and they died.
One day, two deaths. The hands that loved suddenly killed.
And now we are alone. We too will die a painful death—if we ignore the king, forget the law.   60
Remember that we are women.
Remember that the law belongs to men.
This edict, cruel as it is, must be obeyed.
I ask forgiveness. I ask forgiveness of the dead.
I have no power. I must bow to those who have it.
To make a wild and futile gesture makes no sense.

ANTIGONE: I ask nothing of you. Nothing. Even if you *chose* to join me now . . .
I would not permit it. . . . It is too late.   70
Be what you are.
But I will bury Polyneices. I will do what I must do and I will die an honorable death.
I am his family, his kin, and kin will lie by kin.
Mine will be a holy crime.
I must honor not the living but the dead. For I will spend a longer time with them. There shall I lie forever.
As for you . . . dishonor what the gods have honored.

ISMENE: I will dishonor no one. But I cannot resist the rule of law. I cannot.

ANTIGONE: That easy phrase protects you. I will leave you now . . . to bury my brother whom I love.

ISMENE: Oh my sister. I feel nothing but terror. I fear for you.

ANTIGONE: For me? Feel no fear for me! Put your own life in order.

ISMENE: Tell no one of what you are about to do. Keep silence. And I will do the same.

ANTIGONE: No, scream it aloud. Denounce me. If you are silent I will hate you even more. I want the world to know.

ISMENE: Your heart is burning, but what you have to do is cold as ice.

ANTIGONE: I know to whom my love must flow, and flow deep.

ISMENE: If only it could reach him . . . but your love is impossible.

ANTIGONE: When my strength dies, I will die.

ISMENE: But you are wrong from the start . . . to seek what cannot be done.

ANTIGONE: If that is what you believe, I shall be the first to hate you, then the dead, your brother Polyneices, with justice will hate you too. But leave me to my own folly, leave me to the suffering and the terror.
But be sure that I will suffer nothing so shameful as death without honor.

ISMENE: If that is what you believe, then go your way.

14

But mindless is your journey, though you are
    rightly loved by all your family.

CHORUS: Oh Light of the Sun,
    Oh most glorious light that ever shone
    Upon Thebes of the Seven Gates,   100
    Across Dirce's streams,
    Oh eye of the golden sun,
    Oh then did you shine
    Upon the Man from Argos
    With his Gleaming Armor.
    Polyneices!
    Running in unbridled fear now
    In the harsh blaze of your dawn.

    Polyneices!

    He had come in bitter quarrel with his brother.
    Screaming shrill, like an eagle he flew above our
        land.
    Covered with a wing white as snow
    He came, weapons and feathered crests bristling
    In the sun.

    Polyneices!

    He stood above our city's homes, hovered there,
    Spears thirsty for blood,
    A black circle of death.
    And then, before the flames of war could burn our
        tower's crown,
    Before he could slake his jaws' thirst with our
        blood,
    He was turned back.
    The war god screamed at his back.   120
    Thebes rose like a dragon behind him.

    Zeus hates the boasts of a proud tongue.
    And seeing the enemy rolling on like a mighty
        stream

In arrogant clash of gold
He struck the man who rushed to our towers'
    height
Struck him down with a bolt of fire
Before his mouth could scream the cry of victory.

Polyneices!
Traitor!

To the echoing ground he fell, twisting hard,
Fire yet in his hand.
This man, who in mad attack had raged against us
    in his hate.
And the War God, flailing blood,
Marked now one, now another for black death.

Seven Captains stood at the Seven Gates,
Seven against Seven.
They lowered their weapons, yielded to the might
Of Zeus who turns the battle.

All but those brothers in blood,
Two bred of one father one mother,
They alone hurled their spears
And found a common share of death.

Polyneices!
Eteocles!

Now
Victory whose name is Fame
Dances in the joy of Thebes,
City of warriors.

But
Let us forget these rough wars.
Let us worship at the shrines of the gods.
Let us dance through the dark night
And Bacchus will lead us,
God of Thunder, Lord of Thebes.

Ah now comes Creon, son of Menoeceus,
King of Thebes, our new king, appointed by this
    new twist of Fate.
What plan beats in his mind?
Why has he called the Council of Elders?
Why has he summoned us all?   160

CREON: Men of Thebes, the gods, with waves of wrath,
    storm-tossed our Ship of State.
But now they have righted her once more. I have
    summoned you here, from every quarter of the
    city, because I know that I can trust you.
You were loyal to Laius our king.
You were loyal to Oedipus when he restored the
    state.
You were loyal yet again to his descendants when
    he died.

Now it is I who hold the full power of the throne.
    For it descends to me after the double death on
    a single day of the brothers Eteocles and Polyne-
    ices.
Killer and killed were one flesh, and the flesh was
    polluted by spilled blood.
No king can expect complete loyalty from his sub-
    jects until he shows his control over government
    and the law. You cannot know his mind, his soul.
For I truly believe that the man who controls the
    state must have a supreme and moral vision for
    its future. But if he is prone to fear and locks his
    tongue in silence, then he is the worst of all who   180
    ever led this country or could lead it now. I love
    my country. I love no human being more than
    my country.
Zeus is my god and Zeus sees all. I swear that if I
    saw the state headed for disaster I could not
    keep silent. Her safety is our only hope.

17

Nor could I call any enemy of this country my friend.

For when she sails safe upon an even keel, then and only then can we say that we have friends.

These are my principles of government. They will make our city great again.

And that is why I have issued the edict concerning the sons of Oedipus.

Men of Thebes, Eteocles who died defending our city, brave spear in hand, is to be buried with all the honors we bestow on fallen heroes.

But his brother Polyneices who returned from exile to burn and pillage his own father's land, to overturn his native gods, who sought to spill the blood that was his own, who sought to make us his slaves . . . no one in this town may bury him nor mourn for him.

Unburied his corpse will feed wild dogs and carrion birds.

This is my command. Never will I honor the wicked at the expense of the just. The man who is loyal to this city, him I will honor in death as in life.

CHORUS: Creon, you have the right to pass this law. You have the power to rule over the living and the dead, the traitor and the patriot.

CREON: See to it that you enforce the law.

CHORUS: We are old. Entrust this to the young.

CREON: That is not what I mean. Sentries watch the corpse.

CHORUS: Then what would you have us do?

CREON: Give no support to anyone who breaks the law.

CHORUS: I am not a fool. I have no love of death. 220

CREON: And the price *is* death. But there's many a man who has risked his future for money.

(Enter the Watchman)

WATCHMAN: My Lord, I'm not saying that I'm out of breath from running.
No, I didn't exactly put my best foot forward. In fact I stopped to think often enough and nearly went back to where I came from.
I kept thinking: "Go there and you'll pay for it! Idiot! Get going!
For if Creon finds out from someone else it'll be even worse." 230
So I kept on thinking and I kept on slowing down.
I haven't come far but it took long enough. So . . . here I am finally.
I will tell you. It may be nonsense . . . but I'll tell you.
My only hope is that I won't be harmed . . . but what's going to happen . . . is going to happen.

CREON: What has made you so uneasy?

WATCHMAN: Let me tell you first about myself . . . I didn't do it.
I didn't see who did it. It's not fair if I get into trouble.

CREON: You know how to protect yourself. You've built a clever defense.
You have some bad news. Speak.

WATCHMAN: It's terrible. I don't know where to begin.

CREON: Out with it and then be off with you!

WATCHMAN: All right. The corpse . . . well, someone's buried it . . . and . . . gone away . . . dry dust sprinkled on the flesh and all the rituals complete.

CREON: Who dared to do this? Who?

WATCHMAN: I don't know! The ground was hard and
dry . . . there were no signs of digging . . . no
wheel tracks in the dust.
Whoever did this left no trace. Nothing. It was the
guard who had the morning shift who noticed it
first. We felt sick . . . astonished really.
The body was not there as it had been, not *buried*
exactly, just a thin layer of dust, just enough to
put his ghost at rest . . . no footprints of wild animals . . . no dog tracks . . . nothing. The body
was intact.
We began to fight, quarrel, shout at each other.
Guard punched guard.
Accusations flew about. No one could stop it.
Everyone had done it. Nobody had done it. We
were ready to take red-hot iron in our hands to
swear our innocence. We'd walk through fire.
We'd swear by every god we had not done it. We
knew nothing.
Not the when or the where. Finally when we had
talked all questions through, one man spoke up:
it was clear—*you had to be told.*
We all stared at the ground.
But there was no other choice, no way out really.
No way to hide it.
What he said . . . convinced us. We cast lots. I . . .
won. And so I am here.
It's not what I want but I'm here. Not what *you* want
either.
Nobody likes the bringer of bad news.

CHORUS: As I listened, I could only think that this was
some god's doing.

CREON: Stop! You are fools. Old old fools. Do not risk
my anger, for it runs deep.

Some god? Intolerable! The gods care nothing for
this corpse.

Or do you think *they* buried him? . . . since he
treated them so well.

After all, he did come to burn their temples, overturn their images, pillage their land, and break
their laws. Did you ever see the gods honor
wicked men? It is not so.

No. From the beginning I knew that some men in
this city loathed this edict, formed cabals, whis-
pered together, conspired against me. These are
no *subjects.*

These men are not loyal to me.   290

No. These men—oh I can see it, I can see it—they
bribed the guards to do this.

Money! There is nothing in this world that cor-
rupts so much as money.

It destroys the state. It drives men from their
homes. The honest are corrupted.

And all for money.

Money makes evil thrive and wickedness grow fat.   300

Every man who took bribes and helped in this
sealed his own fate there and then.

Now to you. Listen to me carefully. I speak to you
under oath, for I swear before great Zeus whom
I revere: if you don't find the man who laid his
hands upon the corpse and bring him here right
before my eyes, death will not be enough for
you.

I'll string you up alive until you unmask this crimi-
nal. Understand?

Perhaps then you'll learn this lesson: sometimes
greed exacts a heavy price.

Perhaps in the future you'll think twice about the
source of your profit.

You'll see that dirty money destroys more men
than it saves.

WATCHMAN: Can I say something? Or should I just
turn around and go?

CREON: When you open your mouth you irritate me.

WATCHMAN: *Where* exactly . . . ears or heart?

CREON: Why do you anatomize my discomfort?

WATCHMAN: The man who did it hurts your heart . . . I
hurt your ears.

CREON: Talk talk talk! That's all you are fit for!

WATCHMAN: Maybe. But I didn't *do* anything.

CREON: This from you who sold his soul for money.

WATCHMAN: It's terrible when you make a guess and
the guess is simply not true.

CREON: You and your guesses. Clever talk again.
Look, if you don't bring me the men who did this
you'll be *talking* about the punishment that the
money inflicted on you.

(exit Creon)

WATCHMAN: Well, I pray they catch the man! But
whether they do or not . . . that's in the hands of
fate. You've seen the last of *me*!
I didn't expect to get away, no I didn't! But thanks
be to the gods, I'm safe!
(exit)

CHORUS: What a remarkable piece of work is man.
In the tossed waves of winter
He dares the bucking back of the sea
When the swells swirl heavy.

Year in year out he pummels the earth,

Earth, undying, greatest of the goddesses,
Pliant mother,
As the plows turn her soil
And the mules plod on her tireless breast.   340

The birds of the air he nets and brings to earth,
And the wild beasts of the hills.
With nets he traps the tribe of fish from the deep,
Nets fingered with skill.

He is lord over the savage mountain lion,
Masters the long-haired horse and the bull
That has never known the pain of the yoke.

He knows the language of the tongue.
He knows thought that has wings.
He knows the passions that create cities.

And he has found refuge from the arrows
Of rain and hail.
He can do everything. And yet he can do nothing,
Nothing in the face of the death that must come.   360

He has cured disease.
But he cannot cure death.

His mind is rich in thought.
His mind feeds on hope.
But Good comes and Bad comes.

Human laws are frail.
Divine laws live in truth.
Keep the laws of the gods and cities stand high.
Cities fall when arrogant excess keeps court.

Never will the transgressor
Break bread at my table.

(The Watchman enters with Antigone)

CHORUS: My mind splits in pain.
   This is Antigone.

23

Anguished daughter
Of an anguished father.

Oh god, what can this mean?

It cannot be that you have broken the king's law!
You are caught in shame, in shame!

WATCHMAN: This is the woman who did it.
We caught her burying him. Where's the king?

CHORUS: Here. He was waiting.

CREON: Speak to me your Lord. What has happened?

WATCHMAN: One should never make a promise you
can't keep.
You change your mind and you break your word.
My Lord, you threatened me. And I swore I
wouldn't come back.
You terrified me. But I am now a happy man. I
didn't expect to be.
But I am happy beyond dreams.
I'm back. I swore I'd never come, but I'm back and
I've brought the girl.
We caught her burying the dead.
This time we didn't have to cast lots. It was mine for
the taking.
I bring you the news.
O now, my Lord, take her. She's yours. Question
her. Find out the truth.
400   Me? I'm free. You can't bring anything against me.

CREON: Tell me exactly what happened.

WATCHMAN: She was burying him. That's it.

CREON: This is the truth? You understand the conse-
quences?

WATCHMAN: I saw her burying the body. She was break-
ing your law. Enough?

24

CREON: Give me details of how she was caught.

WATCHMAN: It was like this: When we got back there,
terrified by your threats, we brushed the dust off
the corpse. We cleansed the rotting flesh.
And we sat on a mound away from the smell.
We kept each other awake, poking, threatening.
Everyone had to be on the lookout.
We did this for a while. Then it was noon. And hot.
Sun up above.
Out of nowhere came this wind, twisting, whirling,
covering the leaves of the trees.
The plain was filled with spinning dust.   420
We shut our eyes, cursed the gods, and sat there. It
lasted long.
But then suddenly it was gone.
Then we saw the girl.
She screamed, sharp and shrill. Like a bird that has
lost its young.
She began to groan when she saw the naked body,
began to curse the ones who had done this awful
thing.
She took the dry dust in her hands, raised a pitcher
of bronze and poured libations on the corpse,
three comforts for the dead.   430
We saw this and we charged down the hill.
We got her. But she was completely calm. We said
to her:
"You did this and it was you the first time."
She did not say no.
I was so happy.
But it hurt, it hurt.
I'm happy to be found not guilty.
But it hurts to hurt a friend.
However, forget these second thoughts.
I'm glad to be safe.

CREON: You there, you with your head bowed low, do you admit this or do you deny it?

ANTIGONE: I did it. Nothing more.

CREON: *(to the Watchman)* Go! You are free!

CREON: *(to Antigone)* You knew this was against the law? Yes or no?

ANTIGONE: I knew. Of course I knew. Everyone knew.

CREON: And still you did it? You broke the law?

ANTIGONE: It was not god's law. Zeus made no such law.
Nor did Justice who lives with the gods below the earth make it a practice for mankind.
You are a mere mortal. And what you decree is as nothing in the face of the laws of god unwritten and beyond truth.
They live not in the now or in the yesterday.
They live in eternity. They come to us time out of mind.
I am not afraid of any man. Man's power means nothing.
I am afraid of the anger of the gods.
And therefore I have kept their laws.
I knew that I would die. Of course. But your threats meant nothing.
If I die before my time, I think I win.
For if you live in grief such as mine, what is death but a victory?
So there is no grief in death for me. But if I left my mother's son to rot unburied, I would feel grief, but now I grieve not at all.

You may think me a fool. But folly may be in the eye of the beholder.

460

CHORUS: The girl speaks bitter words.
  She is her father's child.
  She fights Fate. So did he.

CREON: People who are proud crack first.
  They shatter like iron forged in hot fire.
  Hard iron splits and slivers in the heat.
  The sliver of a bit reins in the proudest horse.
  Pride makes slaves.
  And this girl is proud, arrogant.
  She broke the law, our city's law.
  She did it. That was the first thing.   480
  Now she boasts of it. She laughs.
  She laughs in my man's face.
  She plays the man. And I am nothing if she wins.
  She is my sister's child. But if she were my own
    daughter she would die.
  She and her sister. For I accuse Ismene too. She
    shared in this . . . this burial.
  Call her out. I saw her in the house. She was no
    longer mistress of herself.
  Sometimes secret plans become revealed before
    the plotters work their evil.
  I loathe too when the workers of evil try to make
    what they do some thing of grace.

ANTIGONE: Do you want more than my arrest and my
    death?

CREON: Nothing. Nothing.

ANTIGONE: What are you waiting for? Nothing you say
    do I agree with.
  I pray I never will.   500
  And I know that nothing I say will touch your
    heart.

  But to bury my brother . . . what could feed my
    glory more?

27

And these men here, they praise what I did but fear
makes them slaves.
But you are free, a king, and you can speak at will.

CREON: That is *not* what they think.

ANTIGONE: That *is* what they think. But in fear they seal their lips.

CREON: You are not ashamed to be the only one who thinks this way?

ANTIGONE: I am not ashamed. When was it a shame to honor your brother?

CREON: But was it not your brother who *killed* him?

ANTIGONE: Yes. My brother. Yes. My mother's son.

CREON: But to bury *him* is a crime, not an act of grace.

ANTIGONE: His dead brother would not say so.

CREON: And you, you make no distinction.

ANTIGONE: No. I do not. For it was a free man who died.

CREON: Making war on his own country! Eteocles died in defense of it.

ANTIGONE: Death is a fair judge. All men are equal.

CREON: The good and the bad are not necessarily equal.

520   ANTIGONE: But who knows if this is eternal truth?

CREON: When a man you hate dies, he does not become your friend.

ANTIGONE: I was born to share in love, not hate.

CREON: Then go down to love the dead below. You are a woman. I am a man . . . that says it all.

CHORUS: Look, Ismene is coming out. She weeps.
For she loves her sister. Her cheeks are torn with
nails of grief.

CREON: You there, poisonous viper! You hid in the
dark of my house and sucked my lifeblood dry.
The pair of you were plotting to overthrow the
throne, but I was blind. Admit it! You did this together. Or will you swear that you knew nothing?

ISMENE: I did it, if she will allow it. I am her partner. I
share the blame.

ANTIGONE: Justice will say no. You had no desire to be
my partner. Nor did I allow it.

ISMENE: The journey with you into pain is what I long
for.

ANTIGONE: Death and the dead know who did this. I
cannot love someone whose love is mere words.

ISMENE: Sister, don't deprive me of honor. Honor for
me is to die with you, bringing glory to the dead.

ANTIGONE: You cannot die with me. You chose to live.
My death's enough.

ISMENE: When you are gone, what love can there be
left?

ANTIGONE: Ask Creon. He is your kinsman and the
one you care for.

ISMENE: Why do you hurt me? It does you no good.   550

ANTIGONE: I hurt too. Even when I laugh at you.

ISMENE: What more can I do for you?

ANTIGONE: Save yourself. I will not begrudge your life.

ISMENE: I am in torment. I cannot share your fate?

29

ANTIGONE: No. You chose life, I chose death.

ISMENE: But I talked to you. I warned you.

ANTIGONE: In some people's eyes, you were right. In others' wrong.

ISMENE: But we both have lost.

ANTIGONE: Be strong. You will live. My breath died long ago. I joined the dead and I will help them.

CREON: Of these sisters, one proved a fool just now. The other was a fool from birth.

ISMENE: Yes, my Lord. When people are in pain, common sense leaves them behind.

CREON: You lost your common sense when you chose to do evil with this evil girl.

ISMENE: What life is there for me to live without her?

CREON: Don't speak of her. She is no more.

ISMENE: Will you kill the future wife of your son?

CREON: Oh, he can plow other fields.

ISMENE: But they were bound together like no other!

CREON: I hate the thought of my son marrying an evil woman.

ANTIGONE: Haimon!—your father robs you of your rights.

CREON: You and your marriage utterly repel me.

CHORUS: You will deprive your son of his bride?

CREON: Death will destroy this marriage.

CHORUS: It is determined then that this girl must die.

CREON: So must you . . . and so must I. *(to slaves)* Move! Slaves, take them inside. They must be

watched. They may be women with no means of
escape.
But even brave men will run away when they see
death coming close.

CHORUS: Happy is the man whose life has never tasted
pain.
For when a house is shaken by the gods
No generation escapes.
The curse lives, ever surging onward,
Like the wave that swells
When the north winds whip the sea
And the black depths spew their sand
And the storm winds rumble off the distant cliffs.

Time out of mind I have seen the sorrows
Of this house, seen them loom and come
Crashing down upon the children.
Grief upon grief.
No generation can escape. A god always strikes.
And now the last light is dimmed.
The last root of the tree of Oedipus   600
Is cut by the bloody knife.
The god of death wills it,
Madness and Fury have made it so.

Zeus, no man can surpass the majesty of your
power.
It is forever young.
Sleep cannot bedim its glory
Nor the endless moving of the months of time.
Yours is the kingdom of Olympus's
Shining heights,
Yours the power and the glory
Time past, now, and forever.
But in the life of man
No pride can escape the anger of the gods.

Their breathless wanderings bring some men
    profit,
Some men mere emptiness.
Ambition stalks the ignorant
620   Until knowledge comes through fire.
This saying holds the wisdom of truth:
"The man who believes the bad to be good
Lives in the grip of the curse of god."
His pleasure is brief, his doom eternal.

My Lord, here is your only son, Haimon.
Does he come in grief for Antigone,
In anger for the loss of his bride?

CREON: We have no need of prophets. We shall know
    soon enough.
My son, you have heard my judgment, my last
    word?
Do you come in fury or in deference to the father
    that you love?

HAIMON: Father, I am your son. You have always set me
    on a straight path.
Your wisdom will always be my guide.
I will not sacrifice that for any marriage.

CREON: My son, your heart tells you true.
Never put anything above your father's will.
A father prays that he will breed sons who live with
    him in duty and obedience, hating his enemies
    and honoring his friends.
But when a son proves good for nothing, what has
    a man bred but trouble for himself and laughter
    for his enemies?
My son, do not let desire for a woman rule your
    mind.
This thing in your arms would soon grow cold
    when you knew you had a wicked woman for a
    wife.

A wicked lover in your bed—what knife could cut
as deep?
No. Spit her out, devil that she is—let her be a
bride in Hell!

She was the only one of all the city to disobey me.
She was caught in the act. I will not be called a
liar—she must die.
She can sing a prayer to Zeus, the god of kinship.
If I allowed disobedience in my own family, I would
have to allow it everywhere.
If a man is honest and fair in the home, he will gain
the public's confidence.   660
I would trust such a man to rule his people well,
even to *be* ruled well.
In the thick of battle, when the hail of spears fall,
he will be there, by your side. But if a man
crosses the law, uses force, makes plans to sub-
vert the power of the state, you will never find I
have a word of praise for him!
Whoever the state has put in power must be
obeyed—in all things, important unimportant,
just and unjust.
Anarchy! There is nothing worse.
Anarchy destroys great cities and hurls great fami-
lies to the dust.
Anarchy breaks the battle lines of great armies.
If men live decent lives it is because *rule of law* is
their protector.
We must protect those who live within the law.
I will not be beaten by a woman. If we must lose, let
it be to a man.
Is a woman to be seen as stronger than we are?

CHORUS: Unless old age has dimmed our wits, we believe that you have spoken sensibly and well.

33

HAIMON: My father, the gods have given men the power to think.

It is the best thing that we have.

I could not find the words to turn your words around.

I have no such skill.

But someone else might argue differently . . . and well.

You cannot know everything that people say or do . . . or how they criticize you.

You frighten them. They are afraid to say things that would annoy you.

But in the darkness I have heard them say that the city grieves for Antigone, grieves for her unjust punishment.

Unjust—to die in shame for what was an act of glory and of justice.

She would not leave her dead brother to lie unburied in the dust, for birds and hungry dogs to make an end of him.

700   She deserves a crown of golden glory.

Beneath the skin of the city that is what you will hear.

My father, your success is my success.

There is no greater pleasure for a son than to see his father prosper and achieve undying respect. And a father wishes the same for his son.

I beg you . . . let your stubbornness die.

You do not alone own truth.

The man who thinks that truth is his alone, who thinks his eloquence and wisdom surpasses all, when his world turns, finds mere emptiness.

A man, intelligent though he be, should never be ashamed of learning more.

His mind must be supple.

When a flood strikes, have you not seen the leaves that submit to the water's rage survive and the

34

resistant trees be swept away? So too the ship
that fights the wind, the sail drawn tight resist-
ing, overturns. She comes home, keel on top.
No. Soften your anger . . . let the winds pass by.   720
I am young, I know, but let me say that it would be
best if men were created with perfect wisdom.
But since this is not so—to learn from others
when they speak good sense is no disgrace.

CHORUS: If your son has spoken to the point, you
should learn from him, and he from you. Both
sides have spoken well.

CREON: At my age I am to be taught by him? I am to be
schooled by a boy?

HAIMON: In nothing that is unjust. True, I am young.
But look not at my age but at what I *do*.

CREON: Even if what you *do* is to respect anarchy?

HAIMON: I have no respect for those who break the
law.

CREON: Is not Antigone so charged?

HAIMON: Your fellow citizens believe her innocent.

CREON: Is the city to tell me how to govern?

HAIMON: Now who is talking like a boy?

CREON: I and I alone give the orders in this city.

HAIMON: It is no city if it belongs to one man.

CREON: The law is that the city is the property of its
ruler.

HAIMON: All alone you would be a fine king—of a de-
serted city.

CREON: *(to Chorus)* He has taken the woman's side.

HAIMON: If you are the woman. It is only you I care for.

CREON: You unspeakable thing you. Contradicting your father!

HAIMON: I must, when you act without justice.

CREON: Is it unjust to respect the duties of my office?

HAIMON: There is no respect. You are trampling on divine law.

CREON: Your mind is poisoned. You have given in to a woman!

HAIMON: I will never give in to what is not right.

CREON: Your whole argument is to protect her.

HAIMON: And you. And me. And the gods under the earth.

CREON: You will not marry her while she is alive.

HAIMON: Then she must die. But her death will bring another death.

CREON: Ah, now your arrogance is in full flood. You threaten me?

HAIMON: It is no threat to try to stop your senseless plans.

CREON: It is you who have lost your senses. And you will regret this argument.

HAIMON: If you weren't my father I would say you were mad.

CREON: Don't call me father. You belong to that woman.

HAIMON: You always want to speak, never to listen.

CREON: Is that so? By god—you will not abuse me like this and get away with it.
(to the slaves) Bring the woman out! Bring her here! 760
She shall die right before his eyes. Die in the bridegroom's arms!

HAIMON: No. Never! She will not die in my arms.
And you will never set eyes on this face again!
Share your madness with others. *(he leaves)* Not with me! Not with me!

CHORUS: My Lord, he is gone. His anger runs deep.
Such a state of mind in the young is dangerous.

CREON: Let him go. Let him think, let him *do* whatever his arrogance feeds him. In any case, the girls must die.

CHORUS: Both of them, my Lord?

CREON: No. You are right. Not the one who did not do it.

CHORUS: And what death have you chosen for Antigone?

CREON: She will be taken where no man walks the desert ground. I will seal her in some hollow cave, still alive. She will be given just enough food to clear the city of the guilt of death. Let her pray there to the only god she honors—the god of Death.
Maybe *he* can save her.
Or maybe she will learn, too late, how futile it is to honor those already dead.

CHORUS: Love! Invincible god! 780
You take whatever we possess.
You sleep in the soft bed

37

Of a young girl's cheeks.
You can cross all oceans,
Move at ease through the wild.
Not the immortal gods,
Not Man who lives but a day
Can escape your embrace.
He who possesses you goes mad.

Even the just man loses his mind.
You twist him into injustice.

You made this quarrel
Of a father and a son,
Provoking shared blood.

Desire shines in the eyes
Of a beautiful bride,
Shines, conquers, and the ordered world
Dissolves.
800   For Aphrodite
Smiles as she kills.

(Antigone enters in chains or under guard)

CHORUS: Ah, now *my* world dissolves. I see Antigone
Going to that chamber where all men sleep.
I cannot hold back my tears.

ANTIGONE: Citizens of this my homeland, you see me
Walking the last steps of my life,
Seeing the last rays of the sun.
Then, never again.
In this life I never heard the music
Of the marriage hymn nor the laughter.

Death, in whose arms all men sleep,
Leads me to the cold waters of Acheron
To be his living bride.

CHORUS: But in honor and bright fame
You walk into the darkness.

Untouched by wasting sickness,
Not slain by savage swords,
Head high and alone among mortals
You walk in life down to the house
Of Death.   820

ANTIGONE: I know the story of sad Niobe,
Know the deep pity of her death.
She too was sheathed in stone,
Choked by the mountain's ivied grip.
As she fades from life she is washed
By endless showers and soft snow.
Her grieving eyes shed eternal tears
That soak her cheeks of stone.
I know her story.
Some god has made it mine.

CHORUS: She was a god and born of gods.
We are mortal and born to die.
But in death, like her, you will find fame
For your life and for your death.
You have gone like a god to your fate.

ANTIGONE: Mock me not. Could you not wait till I had
gone?
Must you throw insults in my face?   840
O gods of my country, oh my city of Thebes!
I call upon Dirce's holy waters,
Upon this sacred land that protects its people.
Look upon me now! Witness my silent unmourned
death.
Remember the law that buries me in a grave of
rock.
I am alive!
But soon I will sleep with corpses
Having a home with neither the living nor the
dead.

CHORUS: You risked all, my child.

39

You climbed to the summit of high Justice.
And you fell, perhaps paying for your father's pain.

ANTIGONE: My father! Oh you touched the deepest
  sorrow of my heart.
  Generations have spilled grief upon grief.
  There is a doom that haunts our house.
  Mother and son breeding life!
860 Breeding death!
  These were my parents, I their child.
  I go now to be with them.
  I did not marry. I did not breed.
  That is my curse.
  My brother, your life, your death
  Have killed me.

CHORUS: You honored the dead.
  We honor you. But power cannot be thwarted.
  You chose. You die.

ANTIGONE. No one weeps for me.
  No one sings a last wedding song.
  I have no friends.
  I walk to death,
  Last light kissing my eyes.
880 Silence!

  (Creon enters)

CREON: You sing your grief. You mourn your own
  death. But you cannot stop its coming.
  Now! Take her. Open the tomb. Put her inside.
  There, all alone, can she choose death or a
  buried life. We are free of guilt. Our hands are
  clean.
  It is time for her to leave this earth.

ANTIGONE: My tomb, Death's bedroom, where I shall
  sleep forever!

Soon I will be with my family, the pale corpses
    whom Persephone welcomed.
I am the last and the most accursed. For I have won
    death before my time.
But I know I shall see again those that I love—my
    dear father, and you my mother, and my brother
    too.   900
I washed your bodies, dressed you for the grave,
    poured the libations at your tombs.
Oh Polyneices! You know the price I pay for cover-
    ing your body.
But in the eyes of the wise what I did was right.
(she turns to the Chorus)
If a child of mine had died or its father, I would not
    have broken the state's decree.
What makes me think this way? If a husband had
    died
I might have found another and then given birth
    again. But my parents are dead, and I can never
    have another brother. That is why I risked my
    life for you, my darling Polyneices. But Creon
    thought that what I did was wrong, dreadful and
    arrogant. And so he marches me away to death.
I will know no marriage bed, hear no bridal song,
    take no husband in my arms nor hold a baby to
    my breast.
Now without a friend, cursed by fate, with life still
    in me
I go to share darkness with the dead.   920

What law of god have I broken? I have done no
    wrong!
Why, in my grief, do I look to the gods for help?
They care nothing for me. I followed the laws of
    god and yet I am condemned for ungodliness. If
    the gods believe this sentence just,

I will learn the truth in death. But if this man here
is the guilty one, may his punishment equal
mine.

CHORUS: The storm winds of her heart are raging still.

CREON: Her guards will regret letting her linger here.

CHORUS: Your words bring death even closer.

CREON: I have no reason to contradict you. *(Creon leaves)*

ANTIGONE: Thebes! My father's city! You gods of old!
I am led away and there is no more time.
Look on me, you men of Thebes.
I am the last of this throne of kings.
Remember my suffering and who inflicted it.
Because I would not break the laws of god.
(Antigone is led away)

CHORUS: My child, my child.
Danae suffered like you,
Locked in a prison of bronze,
Both bedchamber and tomb,
Where the sun could not brush her face.
She was a princess too.
In her, Zeus sowed his seed
In a shower of gold.

Fate moves on relentless.
Man cannot hide.
Not Wealth nor War
Nor castle Walls
Can escape its power.

The son of Dryas, quick to anger,
Raged against the god,
Scorned his power.
Dionysus locked him deep
Within a tomb of rock.

And when his madness slowly dripped away,
He knew that he had mocked the majesty   960
Which now had buried him.
For he had tried to stop the ecstasy
And the fire divine,
Stop the haunting music of the hills.

There is a place where black rocks divide the sea.
Salmydessus.
There the savage god of war
Watched the blood wounds dealt to infant eyes,
Watched the mistress blind her lover's sons,
Plunging the bloody shuttle, gouging deep
Those eyes that never would look on vengeance.

They wept tears of blood,
Wept for the fate that gave them birth,
Wept for their mother, woeful queen.
She was a princess too.   980
Her father, the North Wind, had raised her
In his far-off cave, cradled by storms,
Never to run free in the sun's warm light.
She shares her endless fate with you,
My child, my child.

(enter Teiresias led by a boy)

TEIRESIAS: Men of Thebes, we two have come here together, two with the eyes of one.
   For this is how blind men walk.

(Creon enters)   990

CREON: Teiresias, what news do you bring me?

TEIRESIAS: I will speak, but you must trust a prophet's
   words.

CREON: I have always listened to your advice.

TEIRESIAS: And so you govern our city well.

CREON: I thank you for your help.

TEIRESIAS: But now you walk upon a razor's edge.

CREON: What do you mean? Your words make me shudder.

TEIRESIAS: You will understand when you have heard the meaning of my art.
I sat as of old in the secret haven where I listen to the sacred screams of birds.
I heard bird cries I have never known.
They screeched mad and inarticulate.
I could hear the murderous tearing of their talons, heard the dying of their wings.
I was afraid. I lit a fire of sacrifice upon the altar. The flames refused the flesh and a slimy ooze dripped from the thighs, sputtered, smoked, and died.
Gall spurted from the bladder and became vapor in the air.
1010　The fat dripped, dripped. But did not burn.

The meaning of my art is clear. The ritual failed.
This boy was my eyes. As I am yours.
The city is diseased because of your decision. Every altar in the town is glutted with the spewed-out flesh of Polyneices, regurgitated by dogs and birds . . . the son of Oedipus.
The gods will accept no sacrifice from us, not prayer nor flesh nor flame.
The birds cry in the air, but I do not understand their cries.
For they are gorged with the oozing blood of the dead.
Think about these things, my son. All men make mistakes.

44

But a wise and determined man will change his
course when he knows that he is wrong. He will
cure the sickness.
Pride breeds disaster. Yield to the dead. Why kick a
corpse?
Why kill the dead a second time?
Listen to me. I speak only for your good.
To learn from such a man as me who knows what is
right is not a painful thing, especially if what he
says will do you good.   1030

CREON: Old man! All of you, like archers aiming at a
target, have turned your bows on me.
I know you and your so-called art. You treat me like
a piece of merchandise to be bought and sold.
Make your filthy money, trade in gold from India
or precious metals from Lydia, if that's your busi-
ness.
But you will never bury that corpse.
Not if eagles were to tear his flesh and leave it as an
offering at the throne of Zeus. I will not give him
up. I am not afraid of pollution.
No mortal can pollute the gods. Teiresias, it is a
shameful thing when wise men sell their knowledge, tell lies to make a profit.

TEIRESIAS: Ah, is there no man who can understand or
tell . . .

CREON: Tell what? What trite pearl of wisdom do you
have for us?

TEIRESIAS: . . . no man who knows that wisdom is bet-
ter far than gold?   1050

CREON: And that to be a fool is a most dangerous
thing?

TEIRESIAS: You are the fool. That is your sickness.

CREON: I do not wish to contradict a prophet.

TEIRESIAS: It is too late. You said I lied.

CREON: Prophets! All you think of is money.

TEIRESIAS: Tyrants! All you think of is power.

CREON: Take care. You are talking to a king.

TEIRESIAS: I know. Who helped you to the throne?

CREON: You may be a wise prophet. But you are corrupt.

TEIRESIAS: Stop! You will make me say things that should remain unspoken.

CREON: Speak! But there should be no profit in this for you.

TEIRESIAS: There will be no profit in this for you.

CREON: I will not change. No matter how much money changes hands.

TEIRESIAS: Take what I say to heart. Before the passing of the sun into its depths, you will give corpse for corpse, flesh of your flesh.
You have lost the meaning of the life above and the death below.
You send a living breath into a lifeless tomb.
You keep on earth a body which belongs below, denying it the grave.
The gods above cannot claim him now. Nor you.
He belongs to the gods beneath the earth. And so the Furies will track you down, lurking in the dark they will pounce upon their prey.
1080 You wish to talk of money now?

Soon within your house you will hear the wailing screams of mourning.

46

You left upon the field of war bodies to rot for birds
and dogs to bury with their jaws.
The fathers of these sons will rise against you now.
The stench of your sin will settle on the earth.
Yes. I am an archer. The arrow of my tongue shoots
straight into the heart.
Boy! take me home now.
Let him spill his rage on younger men. Let him still
his angry tongue and learn truth.
(exit Teiresias) 1090

CHORUS: My Lord, these are words of terror. He has
gone.
But his truth remains. I am old, but never yet has
he proven false.

CREON: I know this too. . . . It troubles me. To give in
is hard.
But if my pride breeds stubbornness, then destruction is at hand.

CHORUS: Listen to me, hear what I have to say.

CREON: I am ready. I will listen.

CHORUS: Go! Now! Release Antigone. Tear the rocks
from her tomb.
Bury the waiting dead! 1110

CREON: That is what you think?

CHORUS: There is no time. Gods move as quick as
light.
Destruction falls heavy upon the fools of this earth.

CREON: It is hard to deny what I believe in. But I will
do it.
I cannot fight with Destiny.

CHORUS: You must do this yourself. You cannot leave it
to others.

47

CREON: I am going. Immediately. You! Bring pickaxes
to lay bare the rock.
Come. Bring other men with you. We must reach
the cave that lowers upon our house.
I imprisoned her. Shall I set her free?
The laws of the gods are old, mighty, and a man
must serve them till his death.

CHORUS: Dionysus! God of our city! God of many
names!
Oh help us now!
Semele's golden child!
Born of thunder,
Spinner of Mysteries' Dreams!
Bacchus! You wash your body in our sacred waters.
1120   Women wild with your will within them
Whirl in the night of the seed of dragons!

Help us now!
God of many names!

The nymphs laugh on the hills.
And in the glow of burning torches
You come to us,
You come from the mountains where your ivy
clings
And the waters of Kastalia wash you clean.

We cry your name aloud! *Evoi Evoi.*
You are our god, our Lord of Thebes,
This is your city,
Thebes where your mother birthed and died.

We are sick, diseased.
1140   Heal us now, heal us now.
Come to us across the grieving sea.
You make the stars dance in the black sky of night.
You hear the echo of eternal silence.
Son of Zeus, bring the whirlwind of your ecstasy
And help us now.

MESSENGER: Men of Thebes, ancient city of Cadmus. I can no longer say of any human life that it is good or it is bad. Fate can bless a man, and Fate can ruin the happy or unhappy man in a single day. No man can know what the future will bring. Creon was envied once. His life was good. 1160
He saved this city from its enemies and became its king. He ruled it well.
And he had noble sons. Now everything has gone.
When a man has lost all happiness you cannot say he is alive.
He is a corpse that breathes.
Live your rich life in your palace, sport the trappings of a king, but once your happiness is gone you are nothing but smoke's shadow in the sun.

CHORUS: You talk of kings. What grief do you bring to us?

MESSENGER: They are dead. The living are guilty of their death.

CHORUS: Who died? Who was the killer? Speak!

MESSENGER: Haimon is dead, killed by his own hand.

CHORUS: His own or his father's?

MESSENGER: He killed himself, driven mad by the murder his father had committed.

CHORUS: Teiresias! You saw and told the truth!

MESSENGER: This is my news. You must think of what to do.

CHORUS: Here is Eurydice, Creon's poor wife.
She may have come outside by chance or she may have heard something about her son.

EURYDICE: I heard your words as I was coming out to pray at Athena's shrine.

49

As I moved the bolts which locked the door, I heard of my own pain.

I fainted and fell back into my women's arms.

But speak again. I have known grief before.

MESSENGER: Dear lady, I was there. And I will tell you everything that happened.

I will not try to ease your pain by telling lies. This is the truth.

I followed your husband to the edge of the plain where Polyneices' corpse was lying still. It had been torn apart by wild dogs. . . .

Dear god! We prayed to Hecate and Hades to speed him on his way and turn their anger to mercy. We bathed what was left of him with holy water and burned the flesh on fresh-cut branches.

Then we covered him with a mound of the earth of the land where he was born and turned toward the chamber of rock where Antigone lay, the bride of death. From afar, one of us heard a voice grieving within that accursed place. He ran back to tell Creon.

The king approached. All he could hear were deep groans, the words were unintelligible. He cried out, "Am I a prophet now? Am I walking along the saddest path of my wretched life? I hear my son weeping!

Hurry! Go to the tomb and look inside! Tear the rocks aside.

Look through the crevice and tell me if that is Haimon's voice I hear or if the gods are deceiving me."

We did what we were told. In the far corner of the tomb we saw her.

She was hanging by the neck in a noose made of her own linen veil.

Haimon had his arms around her. He mourned aloud the death of his bride, her departure from this life . . . and cursed his father.

When Creon saw him he moaned aloud, moved toward him, and called out, "What have you done? My son, speak to me.

What is in your mind? Your suffering is killing you. Come out to me. I beg you. Come to me!"

Haimon looked at him, his eyes on fire. He spat in his father's face and then said not a word.

Suddenly he drew his sword and lunged at his father. Creon leapt aside.

In a fury Haimon turned the sword upon himself, fell upon it hard.

The blade entered his side, half its length pierced his flesh.

Still conscious he crawled toward the girl and gently put his arms around her.

Blood spurted from his mouth and stained her white cheek.

Corpse lay upon corpse. This was their bridal bed.   1240

The hymns of their marriage are now sung in the halls of death.

He did not listen to good sense, and in his death he is a lesson for all mankind.

(Eurydice runs into the palace)

CHORUS: The queen left without a word! What do you make of this?

MESSENGER: I do not know what to think. We can only hope that she needs to grieve in private with her women, away from the general public.
She knows what is best.

CHORUS: Perhaps. But her silence weighs upon me more than any cry of grief.

MESSENGER: You may be right. I too fear the silence.
I will go inside and see if in the wildness of her
heart she means to harm herself. *(Messenger
exits)*

CHORUS: Here is the king. Look, he bears his grief in
his arms, brings home his own damnation.

1260   CREON: Oh the sins of my wicked heart!
The murdering crimes of my heart!
You see before you the killer and the son he killed.
What price to pay for my love of the city!
My son, you died too young, too young.
I was the fool, not you. You died in innocence.

CHORUS: You have learned truth. Too late, too late.

CREON: I learned it in my tears. Some god has struck
me down.
Crushed me with the weight of heaven's curse.
He drove me to this madness,
Pressed his heavy foot upon my happiness.
Oh the sorrow, the pity!

(the Messenger returns)

MESSENGER: You hold one sorrow in your arms. But
there is more.
1280   And you will find it in the palace.

CREON: What further suffering can there be?

MESSENGER: The queen is dead. The mother of this
poor child.
Her wounds bleed still.

CREON: Hades! Where all men must travel, you have
destroyed me now.
I weep in the horror of your words.
I was dead and you have killed me again.

Aaaagh! My son, the queen are dead . . . death upon death.

(the doors open and the body of the Queen is revealed)

CHORUS: Now you can see. All is in the light.

CREON: Yes, I look upon the second anguish of this
day.
What further pain can strike me now?
Just now I held my son in my arms. And now I look
upon the body of my wife.
Oh pity the mother, pity the son!   1300

MESSENGER: By the altar she fell upon the sword and
her eyes embraced the darkness.
She moaned for Megareos, her firstborn, and for
this child here.
And as she died she cursed you, the killer of her
children.

CREON: Aaaagh! Fear courses through my veins.
Will no one turn their sword on me? Pity this piti-
ful man by killing him!

MESSENGER: She held you guilty of the death of both
her sons.

CREON: Tell me once more of her death.

MESSENGER: When she heard of Haimon's death she
thrust the blade through her heart.

CREON: The guilt *is* mine, all mine. I killed you! Shout
it loud!
Take me in, take me from the sight of men. I am
nothing now.

CHORUS: That is good, if anything can be so called.
It is best to make a quick end of our sorrows.

CREON: Let me go, oh let me go. May my death be soon.
Let me never see another day, another dawn.

CHORUS: That is in the future. We must deal with the present.
What will be is out of our hands.

CREON: All my heart was in that prayer.

CHORUS: Pray no more. No man can escape what Fate has in store for him.

1340 CREON: Lead me away, the man who in his madness killed . . . oh you my son and you my wife.
I did not mean to do it!! Where can I turn, where lay my head to rest?
Whatever my life has touched has turned to dust. A cruel Fate has struck me down.

(Creon and his attendants go into the palace)

CHORUS: Wisdom it is that breeds happiness.
The gods take what is theirs.
The words of a proud man are always punished.
Wisdom comes to the old.